We Recycle

Torrey Maloof

Consultants

Sally Creel, Ed.D.
Curriculum Consultant

Leann Iacuone, M.A.T., NBCT, ATC
Riverside Unified School District

Jill Tobin
California Teacher of the Year
Semi-Finalist
Burbank Unified School District

Image Credits: Cover & p.1 Jupiterimages/Getty Images; p.12 Randy Faris/agefotostock; p.4 Simon Marcus/agefotostock; pp.7 (top), 23 Blend Images/Alamy; p.8 Blickwinkel/Alamy; pp.10–11 PhotoAlto/Alamy; p.11 (top) Tetra Images/Alamy; p.2 Allen Donikowski/Getty Images; p.17 Cultura/Getty Images; pp.14–15 Steve Debenport/Getty Images; p.15 (top) Will Giles-The Exotic Garden/Getty Images; pp.6–7 (bottom), 9, 19, 24 iStock; pp.20–21 (illustrations) Janelle Bell-Martin; all other images from Shutterstock.

Library of Congress Cataloging-in-Publication Data

Maloof, Torrey, author.
  We recycle / Torrey Maloof; consultants, Sally Creel, Ed.D., curriculum consultant, Leann Iacuone, M.A.T., NBCT, ATC, Riverside Unified School District, Jill Tobin, California Teacher of the Year Semi-Finalist, Burbank Unified School District.
    pages cm
  Summary: "People throw away a lot of trash. But we do not want Earth to be covered in trash. We need to help keep Earth clean. Reduce, reuse, and recycle to do your part!"— Provided by publisher.
  Audience: Grades K to 3.
  Includes index.
  ISBN 978-1-4807-4573-5 (pbk.)
  ISBN 978-1-4807-5063-0 (ebook)
1. Recycling (Waste, etc.)—Juvenile literature. I. Title.
  TD794.5.M357 2014
  363.72'82—dc23
                                        2014013189

Teacher Created Materials

5301 Oceanus Drive
Huntington Beach, CA 92649-1030
http://www.tcmpub.com

ISBN 978-1-4807-4573-5

© 2015 Teacher Created Materials, Inc.
Made in China
Nordica.082015.CA21501181

Table of Contents

Where Does It Go?

You have a piece of trash, so you throw it away.

This girl throws away her trash.

But where does the trash go?

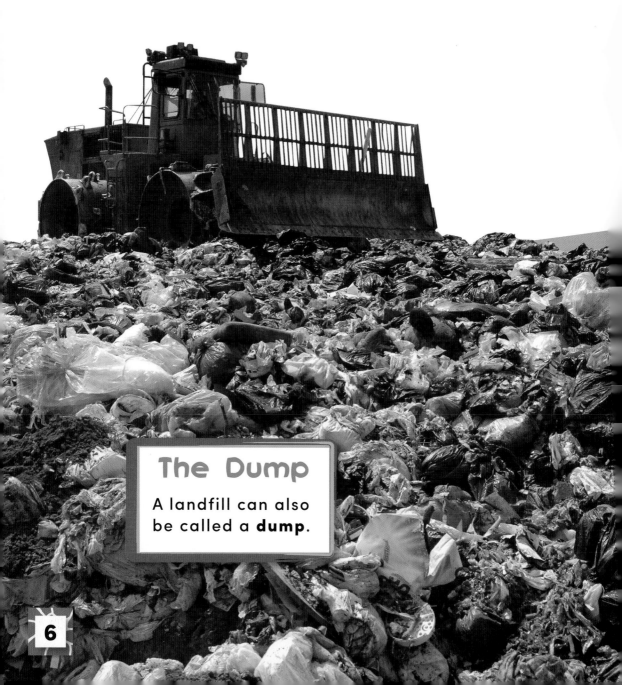

The Dump

A landfill can also be called a **dump**.

Most trash goes to a **landfill**.

More trash is brought to a landfill.

What will happen when there is no more room for landfills? Where will the trash go then?

The trash is spilling out of this can.

Reduce, Reuse, Recycle!

We do not want Earth covered in trash, so we must work hard to keep it clean.

These boys clean up a beach.

These kids pick up trash.

One way to help do our part is to **reduce** trash. This means to make less trash.

Reduce trash by using cloth bags for shopping.

Better Bottles

Pour your drinks in bottles you can wash and use again.

We can also **reuse** items. This means to use an item more than once.

Give clothes that are too small to someone who can wear them.

DONATIONS

Something New

You can reuse old things to make new things. This is a wind chime made out of old spoons and forks!

A great way to help is to **recycle** (ree-SAHY-kuhl). This means to turn one thing into another.

These things can be recycled.

These kids help sort things that can be recycled.

Help Earth

It is important that we keep Earth clean. It is our only home! What will you do to help?

This boy helps by recycling.

This family recycles plastic bottles.

Let's Do Science!

What happens when we reuse old containers? Try this and see!

What to Get

- ⭕ clean, used plastic container
- ⭕ glue or string
- ⭕ paint or decorations
- ⭕ scissors

What to Do

Look at the container. Think of something that you can make out of it. It may be a toy or an animal. It may be a place to keep things.

2 Have an adult help you use scissors, glue, or string to make your new item. Then, paint or decorate it.

3 Talk about what you made. What would happen to the container if you did not make something new out of it?

Glossary

dump—a place where trash is taken and left

landfill—a place where trash is buried under the ground

recycle—to take old items and use them to make new items

reduce—to make something smaller in size, amount, or number

reuse—to use something again

Index

Your Turn!

Recycle It!

Label three boxes *paper*, *glass*, and *plastic*. For one week, place trash that can be recycled into the boxes. How many items can you recycle in one week? Make a list!